Jedi Manual
Intermediate
The Path of Truth

By Matthew Vossler

Jedi is a trademarked name used by George Lucas referencing his characters in the Star Wars movies and stories. My use of Jedi in this manual refers specifically and only to those practitioners of Jediism; a recognized religion.

Oaklight Publishing, LLC
4306 Independence Street
Rockville, MD 20853
USA
http://oaklightpublishing.com

ISBN 978-0-9826533-9-5
First edition: May 2011

Contents

Sometimes when I lose, I really win . . . .

Preface

The first book of this series, *Jedi Manual Basic, Introduction to Jedi Knighthood*, introduces to the reader the requirements for becoming a Jedi Knight. These are examples of how others have accomplished becoming a Jedi and what it means to be a Knight. Optional projects are assigned that are basic "tests" along one's path to becoming a Jedi Knight with the goal of ultimately becoming a master.

In *Jedi Manual Basic*, I cover some Jedi philosophy, religious aspects, and hands-on techniques that Jedi Knights can use. An important element of the first book is the identification of the twelve paths of the Jedi Knight.

In *Jedi Manual Intermediate, The Path of Truth*, I focus on our study. If "Basic," is a summary of the many aspects, "Intermediate," is a focus on the essential.

In this book I am not going to provide you with answers, but questions with which to derive the answers you seek. These questions are designed to help you delve deep within yourself and discover what it means on a personal level to be a true Jedi. And, with these truths the Jedi are armed to make the world a better place for themselves and for others.

Don't mistake the brevity of this manual or any of its chapters as indications of usefulness. There is a movement among the publishing industry, driven by the demands of the reading public, to make available shorter works that are not puffed up with extra words that are designed to fatten up the spine of the book in order to charge more money.

The idea of this and other books like it is that it is worth just as much to a reader to not waste their time with repetition and puffed up writing, but to make available the essential information. In our busy lives, this concept is not to be underestimated.

Chapter One: Why be a Jedi? What stops me?

"This burden has been appointed to you... and if you do not find a way, no one will."
–JRR Tolkien

Maybe you picked up this book because you already consider yourself a Jedi, or perhaps you are curious to learn more about this new religion. By religion, I mean any number of things, for Jedi and Jediism encompasses philosophy, religion, a way of life or thinking discipline, and more.

Some Jedi do not consider their path religious while some do. Most who call themselves Jedi Realists embrace the aspects of Jediism that teach how to use the Force or Universal energy and combine learning and practicing of many Eastern, alternative, and New Age techniques for self-enhancement, personal growth and healing of themselves or others.

Some Jedi more or less embrace the fullness of the ideas laid out in the Star Wars literature and films, including the notion of mentoring a Padawan and practicing swordsmanship with "light-sabers." Some Jedi are solo while many seek out a group to join with.

Let's assume for a moment that you already began your Journey towards becoming a Jedi Master. You've read and studied, practiced and taught, but you have reached a plateau; you are stuck in a rut and aren't learning or progressing more. Perhaps your group disbanded, or your Padawan or Master has moved on. What is the next step?

The next step can be two-fold. When we find ourselves in a rut or even backsliding, the first step can be to ask the question, why did I originally want to be a Jedi; why did I begin this path of the wise and powerful Wizard?

Maybe originally we followed a romantic notion that it would be cool to be a Jedi and do those things that happen in the movies and books. Or maybe our reasons were more practical. We needed healing and sought to use the power of a connection to the Force to improve our life situation. We were being bullied or couldn't get ahead and reach the goals we set for ourselves long ago. Or perhaps the religious or philosophical ideas espoused by Yoda, Obi-Wan, and the others resonated so closely with our own ideas about life, that it was just natural to take on the mantle of the Jedi and follow a path that added more to what we already believed, and we wanted to join with likeminded individuals.

Whatever the reasons, let's reflect on them now. Ask yourself some questions. The mere act of asking questions demands an answer. If that answer is not forthcoming, keep asking the questions until the answers come. Also reflect on why you might be stuck and progress is stalled. Was what I wanted to get out of it achieved or even achievable? Have my beliefs changed or the landscape of my life altered in such a way that Jediism no longer has a place for me or I'm just too busy with other commitments and activities? If I am backsliding; losing motivation in personal power or integrity, what are the reasons for it? Why? What are the reasons behind this happening? Do I need the council of a professional psychologist or just to talk things through with a trusted friend?

Write down in a journal your own questions regarding this. After each question you write down, skip a space or two for the answers to be written later. Then, as the answers come to you, write them down. The answers may not come immediately. Meditate each day during this process. Keep this book or your journal handy, for the answers won't all come at once. It might take you a week or a month to find even the right questions and then their answers. Keep in mind that the path of the Jedi is one of the most difficult a human can take.

_____

_____

_____

_____

_____

_____

_____

_____

_____

_____

_____

_____

_____

_____

_____

_____

_____

_____

_____

_____

_____

_____

_____

_____

_____

_____

_____

_____

_____

_____

_____

_____

_____

_____

_____

_____

_____

_____

_____

_____

_____

_____

_____

_____

_____

_____

_____

_____

_____

_____

_____

_____

_____

_____

_____

_____

_____

_____

_____

_____

_____

_____

_____

_____

_____

_____

_____

_____

_____

_____

_____

_____

Once you are satisfied that you've thoroughly investigated your feelings and thoughts about why you want to be a Jedi and why you might be stalled in your pursuit, it's time to ask one more question:

Does it still make sense for me to be a Jedi?

Meditate on this for at least a week. An honest answer is what we are after. After reflecting for a time, you will know whether or not pursuing the path of the Jedi is right for you. If it isn't the path for you, then congratulations; coming to know this has been more than worth the price of this book.

However, if this path is right for you, and you are indeed in a rut regarding your progression towards mastery, then we must address the questions surrounding why you are at this impasse. If you are progressing nicely, there is still much for you to consider within the pages of this book.

We should start addressing the question: What is stopping me in my path of becoming a greater Jedi?

This may be, by far the most difficult question yet to answer. For we, as humans, often lie to ourselves and come up with a thousand excuses to explain our shortcomings and failings. But we must understand that *we* are doing this. This is an essential part of a Jedi's training. If we cannot see how we rationalize our behavior, then we won't get far in determining the answer to the question of what is holding us back.

If the case is that you do not perceive any rationalizations, then one of two things may be happening. One possibility is that you are rationalizing and cannot yet see this or two, you are not rationalizing and can already admit that you are completely responsible for anything and everything that is stalling your progress.

If you do take full responsibility, congratulations; you are ahead of many in a practical, spiritual sense. If it is the first instance holding you back, here is an easy way to spot your rationalizations: Identify what it is you want that you are not getting, and then examine what it is that is stopping you from attaining it and why. What excuses are you telling yourself and/or others? Who are you blaming for your problems? If you are not meditating, for instance, what do you say to yourself? Do you say, "I'm not meditating because it's too hard", or "I don't have the time"? Do you say that the kids or the roommates make so much noise that it's too difficult for you to concentrate?

Whatever your reasons, know that they are merely excuses. Even those who are approaching Jedi mastery fall into this trap from time to time.

So, what is holding me back from being a better Jedi?

Maybe the answer seems simple. We don't meditate and we don't take the time to do the things that keep us in contact with the Living Force. Let's assume that you are committed to becoming a great Jedi master. Let's also assume that your excuse is that you don't have time for meditating and staying in contact with the Force. So the more difficult aspect of the question is why do we not have time for these things?

I've often heard from motivational gurus that we don't have time to do the things that we know are good for us because we don't *make* the time for them. People sell books and give seminars on how to make time for yourself. They say that if it's important to you, you'll find the time or make the time, and this is true. But we as Jedi, by definition, have a higher purpose; it is the essence of the Jedi to better ourselves and to improve life for those around us. By definition we are committed to our goals.

We cannot truly call ourselves Jedi if we are not completely dedicated to these principles. We are called to become Masters, those who don't shy away from difficult tasks. We are the courageous ones, those that others look to and look up to.

If you've gotten this far, then you have likely identified as a Jedi, and if so, you MUST take the time to meditate and learn the ways of the Force. Jedi are committed to helping others and creating a better world. If you don't discipline yourself through meditation, you cannot honestly call yourself a Jedi. It's that simple.

You and I are on a journey—we are on the Path of Truth!

It's time to take out another piece of paper or utilize the space provided below. Write down all the things that are stopping you from progressing in your path. Note each obstacle and skip three lines before identifying the next issue.

Example: "I do not meditate every day."

In the line beneath that admission, I write: "Because my day is full of too many activities, I don't have time to meditate."

Finally, in the third and forth lines, write all the things you can do to change this.

Your response might be: "I will find the time by watching less television and spending less time chatting on the phone or texting with my friends. Or, I can use downtime at work during break or while sitting in a traffic jam. I can take ten minutes off my lunch period to sit at my desk and practice a short meditation, or I can spend less time playing online games. I will spend less time on the internet. I will drive to work or school with the radio *off*." This isn't a recommendation to meditate while driving, but more quiet time facilitates higher awareness in general.

Perhaps one of the challenges you've identified is that you have a disability. Maybe you do not have the use of your legs, or have a diagnosis of depression. I know Jedi who deal with these things and work around them.

When we take what used to be excuses and turn them into challenges to overcome, we've made a big step towards taking responsibility for our life. Taking full responsibility for our actions and life situations is what the path of truth is all about. For Jedi mastery, it is essential.

What if your reason for stalled progress is that you cannot find a way to practice your energy work or find another Jedi to teach you healing techniques? Write these challenges down and actively seek to unearth solutions.

If the answers don't come immediately, keep asking the questions. Sleep on it, give it a week or two, go for long walks, or seek the council of a trusted friend, or mentor in your Jedi Order.

_____

_____

_____

_____

_____

_____

_____

_____

_____

_____

_____

_____

_____

_____

_____

_____

_____

_____

_____

_____

_____

_____

_____

_____

_____

_____

_____

_____

_____

_____

_____

_____

_____

_____

_____

_____

_____

_____

_____

_____

_____

_____

_____

_____

_____

_____

_____

_____

_____

_____

_____

_____

_____

Now that we have completed our lists of challenges and their possible solutions, it's time to put our solutions to the test. Try each solution and monitor your results. If any of the solutions are not working, identify the reason by putting to use the deductive skills we have learned thus far.

If the solution you came up with is impractical or unattainable, re-think your solution and try that. Keep trying until you find one that works. It's easy to give up on things that are frustrating, but as Jedi, we know that giving up is not the path we've chosen.

What if a solution doesn't work because we aren't following through? Again, we must go back and examine why. Do we get discouraged or lose interest because of depression? Maybe it's the opposite; something wonderful is happening (either with work, school or a relationship) and taking up most of our energy and time.

If the reason is depression, it might be time to seek a professional trained in addressing such personal issues. If, for example, it's because we just started dating someone new, someone we may be in love with, and we just can't think of anything else, then understand what is happening and remember previous commitments.

Don't put others needs before your own. You are of no help to anyone else if you haven't ensured that your own needs are being met.

Also keep in mind that during a short term emergency or family crisis, it may not be the the time to stubbornly adhere to a meditation schedule. Take care of the crisis first and when things stabilize, get back on track with your spiritual goals.

Chapter Two: The Struggle with Dark Forces

Now we've identified that we are indeed Jedi on a path to mastery, and we have begun to come to terms with what holds us back.

We have decided on some ways to overcome our personal obstacles and have begun progress once again, or for the first time. When this is going on for me, I am happy. This may be when we humans are happiest; we are in the process of improving ourselves.

This euphoric sense of being may go on for a while and the path may begin to feel easy. Be careful, though. It's human nature to become complacent when things go well. Be assured that life always has other ideas. Problems have a way of developing or returning. Dark forces and negativity rain upon us constantly and if we aren't aware and prepared for this truth, we can become caught up in it and swept away from our path.

Maybe our boyfriend or girlfriend decides to dump us, or we are robbed or violated. Perhaps it's more like a temptation that presents itself and entices us to act against our own better judgment.

It is natural to encounter these kinds of situations and the feelings they conjure up, but the dark path is not that of a Jedi. We often become entangled with darkness, but it's important to remain steadfast in our path, to persevere against, and overcome darkness, even if we have to go through the process time and time again. When we find ourselves caught up in this cycle, we naturally feel discouraged. I've known people who've fallen back so many times, that it seems like a miracle when they finally overcome their personal demons.

I myself have encountered the same kinds of dark forces so many times, it seemed like I'd never surmount them. Over time, I've learned that although the darkness often comes from outside ourselves, it is only from within that we can expel it from our lives. I did not learn this from a book; it came from experience. It is this kind of learning that make us powerful Jedi. It is experiential learning that allows us to become qualified and powerful mentors of other Jedi.

This is not to say that we do not rely on things outside ourselves in our quest to expel darkness. Some things cannot be done without the aid of others in our life or a connection to the Living Force, or God. An experienced Jedi knows when to deal with a problem by him or herself, using the Force, and when to ask for help from others. True humility is based on this kind of wisdom—the wisdom and humility to ask for help when we cannot overcome an obstacle by ourselves.

Even so, after receiving help through the Force and others, darkness can only be expelled from within. We are the ones ultimately responsible. Only we can make the decision to change and not go back.

Now I want to revisit our list of ways to overcome what has been holding us back. I am now going to offer you some tools that will be useful as you work towards Jedi mastery. First we have to learn about the basic tool of the Jedi.

Jedi speak of using the Force. Having a relationship with the Force is central to the life of a Jedi. The Force is what sustains us, and gives us courage and strength. But what exactly is the Force?

Many Jedi get hung up on this question and have endless discussions or debates online or face to face with other Jedi about what it is and how to utilize it. But the truth about the Force, just like finding the strength to change, ultimately can only come from within. By quieting the mind through meditation, we find the truth and meaning of life and the Force. This is one of the best ways to overcome dark forces that keep us from our goal of mastery.

The first tool I want to offer is a partially guided meditation. But before I get to that, let's explore meditation in general.

Meditation is usually described as a quieting of the mind. Some say that prayer is talking to God, while meditation is listening to Him or Her. Note that I said Her. That wasn't a mistake on my part. For me, the Force is both feminine and masculine.

Again, meditation is a quieting of the mind.

When we stop the running dialogs that constantly go on when we are thinking, which for me is very often, we open our minds to insights and suggestions that do not occur otherwise.

Indeed the Force *can* talk to us when we allow it to. Through meditation we can receive benefits that have been verified by scientific studies—lower blood pressure, improved mental and physical health, and even a fresher, more youthful appearance. We have more energy, patience, and stamina. We are calmer and have a feeling of wellness. We find it easier to enjoy life and we are inspired.

A common form of meditation is to sit quietly and undisturbed while concentrating on controlling our breathing. When a thought enters our mind, we tell ourselves to *stop* and return to quietness. Don't be concerned if you have to do this over and over again. Eventually the thoughts will subside and we will gain control. This is done for a prescribed amount of time.

We can also count our breaths from one to four and then back to one again. The counting interrupts the endless thought chatter.

Another way to meditate is to use what is known as a mantra. A mantra is a sound, syllable, word, or group of words that are considered capable of creating transformation." We sit quietly and repeat the mantra over and over either in our minds or out loud.

Some people equate exercise or long walks with meditation. Some of the famous philosophers found their best inspirations while taking long walks away from the noise of others.

Take some time to experiment with meditation. If it is convenient, put down the book now and try out one of the techniques I've mentioned. After you've done this, write in your journal about the method you used and your results. If you don't keep a journal, it is a good idea to start one.

There are many guided meditation tapes, CDs, podcasts, video casts, and the like, already on the market. These work for some people and are worth investigating. I've used many of them and while they have their benefits, I've found that meditation works best for me when I do it without listening to a guided meditation and utilize one or any combination of the techniques I've described.

The next tool I'm going to give you is what I call a partially guided meditation; that is, I'm going to provide you an outline for you to put into practice yourself. You won't just be passively listening to a voice with pretty music, but will be doing most of the work yourself. I will incorporate these techniques, which, when combined, are almost sure to yield very consistent and positive results.

Partially Guided Meditation

I call this a partially guided meditation because I suggest that you tailor the meditation to what works for you. The meditations will change and evolve as you do more of them. In this section as well as in appendix A, I provide a number of meditation ideas for you to pick and choose from.

Next, choose a time when you will not be interrupted by the phone, children, husband, wife, friends, and choose a place where you will have quiet for at least 20 minutes. It doesn't need to be where you will be guaranteed 100% silence, but relative privacy is required.

Now get comfortable sitting in a soft chair, sofa, or the floor. Sit with your spine straight and be sure not to cross your arms or legs. Rest your arms on your thighs with your palms up provided doing so does not make you uncomfortable.

Close your eyes and silence the chatter in your mind, replacing it with something relaxing and peaceful. Maybe a song you heard earlier in the day is playing over and over in your head.

Focus on your breathing. If thoughts persist, say silently or out loud, "stop," and go back to quietness and being aware of your breathing. Begin to count your breaths—one, two, three, four, one, two, three, four, again and again. The counting, as I've said, will interrupt even the most stubborn of intrusive thoughts.

Switch back and forth between these two techniques, the "stop" thoughts technique, and the counting to four techniques.

When you achieve quietness, stay with it as long as possible. When noise returns, observe them without judgment against yourself or the process. Become aware of what is behind your thoughts. It was once said, "I think, therefore I am." But what is it that is listening to your thoughts? What is observing them? It is is your true self, your awareness, your connection to the all, your connection to the Force. You are the Force individualized.

Once you become aware of, and acknowledge your thoughts, let them go.

What I want you to do now is to picture yourself inside a giant octahedron. An octahedron is two pyramids back to back. Visualizing yourself inside one of these (see figure No. 1) will add a measure of protection from any dark forces that might be seeking to interrupt your meditation. This visualization can also add to the quality of your meditation.

Perform this visualization while continuing the "stop" thoughts and counting breaths techniques. Bring your awareness to your environment, nothing in particular, but all of it at once. Continue this for another two minutes.

Now I will introduce another powerful meditation technique to add to the mix.

Picture a ball of brilliant white light. See it about three feet in front of you, slightly above the level of your head. See the brilliant ball of light slowly spinning and pulsating or radiating.

Now visualize the ball of light moving towards you, then see it entering your body. It is in you now. You are now the light and this light is radiating outward from you into the room.

Streams of light are shooting out of you into the world. You are light and the light is you, radiant in your splendor.

Continue to use the other techniques as needed and now slowly roll your eyes up and slightly back. Do this as long as it is comfortable and continue meditating for another five or ten minutes.

To come out of the meditation, sit forward and slowly open your eyes. Notice how you feel.

When I do this, I often go from a state of daily agitation to a state of relaxation and of well being that defies explanation. It's like magic! This feeling sometimes can last all day and when this ritual is done every day, the benefits are outstanding.

Figure No. 1

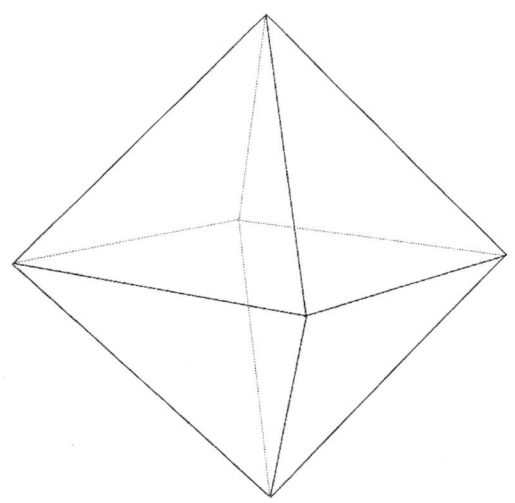

I've just given you a powerful tool for health and connection to the Force. You should also have gotten a glimpse of your true self.

Become familiar with these methods by reading them over a few times and practicing. It is up to you now to practice this or your own version of meditation daily. If you miss a day or two, do not let this get you down or in the way of stop you from getting back on track.

Chapter Three: Honesty – The Spark of Light

We've explored some of the basic and essential aspects to the life of a Jedi. Connecting with the Force, and becoming honest about who is really in control of our actions and life situations.

For the Jedi intermediate, taking full responsibility for one's self is the key to moving forward towards the goal of mastery. No true Jedi makes excuses or blames others for their own faults and failings. To do so is to be a child and is not the hallmark of one aspiring to master one's life.

If you have yet to reach the place where you can no longer blame others and stop making excuses, you may want to cease reading now and revisit the first two chapters of this text. Take more time to explore yourself and dig deeper into what it is you truly want to accomplish in this life.

In this chapter, we'll dig deeper into the issue of honesty and cover some examples of the benefits of honesty as well as some of the hazards of dishonesty. I will provide at the end of this chapter yet another device to help you arrive at this place—becoming honest with yourself. Honesty is the cornerstone for progressing through the rest of this book and moving onto what comes next in this series, *Jedi Mastery: Path of the Immortals*. Honesty is the first real requirement of a Jedi. Without honesty, there can be no further progress.

If you have read the first book in this series, *Jedi Manual Basic: Introduction to Jedi Knighthood*, you may recall some of the things that define a knight. Such traits as honor, valor, courage, and many other qualities of good character are listed.

In this book, I want to emphasize honesty, as the title says we are on the path of truth. What follows now are some examples of the benefits of being honest with others, but especially with yourself.

My path of Jediism began twenty five years ago at the time of this writing. This is when I stopped drinking too much alcohol and began walking a much more spiritual road.

For me, it was the beginnings of becoming a Jedi. When faced with personal obstacles, the first key to change is getting honest with yourself.

By being honest with yourself and seeking help from the Force and other people in your life, a Jedi can surmount even the most challenging personal problems.

Take as another example, the Jedi who is mentoring someone who is not as advanced. What happens if the mentor is not completely honest with his or her mentee? Any number of things could happen. One could be that the mentee points out the dishonesty and they both learn from the experience. Another possibility is that the mentor represents themselves as an authority on a subject that they are not, and the mentee relies on the advice or guidance, only to fail and perhaps even put themselves in danger.

What if a Jedi overstretches their own skill in some matter and ends up getting hurt or hurting someone else? In this case, the Jedi hasn't been honest with him or herself regarding personal limitations.

Or what happens when a Jedi lies to their employer, gets caught, and loses their job? This is not an honorable example to others, and as Jedi, honor is important. Others look to us and look up to us, and we do not let them down. If we do, then we must be honest enough to admit that it is through our own fault and go back to the basics of working on becoming more honest.

Take out a pen and your journal to write down some examples of when you have been honest and how that has made a positive difference in the situation and also write down some examples of when you've been less than honest and what the consequences were, if any. If you don't want to commit such things to paper, just think about them and go over them in your head a little bit each day for a week.

_____

_____

_____

_____

_____

_____

_____

_____

_____

_____

_____

_____

_____

_____

_____

_____

_____

_____

_____

_____

_____

_____

_____

_____

_____

_____

_____

_____

_____

_____

_____

_____

_____

_____

_____

_____

_____

_____

_____

_____

_____

_____

_____

_____

_____

As we go on to the next chapter, "finding your path," and the one's after that, you will discover that these exercises in honesty are worth the trouble and thought. Finding the right path or paths for you is best done coming from a completely honest place.

Assessing your strengths, talents, and desires honestly will put you on the right path(s) to begin with and could save you the time of going down a dead end path, only to have to start over. Of course sometimes this is necessary for our learning, so take what is written here in the same way you are advised to approach everything, with flexibility.

Chapter Four: Finding Your Path

In *Jedi Manual Basic*, I identified what I call the twelve paths of Jedi. A Jedi is a master if they achieve mastery in one or more of these paths. The paths are general categories, and together they encompass just about any skill, career, or activity that a Jedi could find themselves involved in. If you know of an activity that does not fit in one of the twelve categories, that's fine too. This book is not intended to be the last word on Jediism.

Here is the list again. Note that they all have the same ultimate goal of using the chosen path(s) to better serve others. This is the underlying purpose of Jedi; to serve others. The dark path, in contrast, is concerned with forcing or coercing others to serve you.

Read over these twelve paths and try to identify one or more of them that either you have already embarked on, or that you feel drawn to.

The Twelve Paths of a Jedi Knight

- Training and practice in meditation
- Training and practice in martial arts
- Training and practice in the healing arts
- Training and practice in psychic awareness and social graces
- Training and practice in mediation, diplomacy, and peacemaking
- Training and practice in the Jedi philosophy and religion
- Training and practice in teaching, coaching, and mentoring
- Training and practice in practical skills for defending and protecting others
- Training and practice in gentle and objective deliberation, persuasion, and debate
- Training and practice in literary and theatrical arts
- Training and practice in working with energy and the supernatural
- Sustained pursuit of knowledge and wisdom and attaining a good measure thereof

The goal: To become a master in one or more of these areas in order to be of service to others and society.

Now that you have read over the list and given it some thought and perhaps some meditation, what jumps out at you regarding your own situations, experience and skills? Maybe it's more than one. Many Jedi are involved in several categories and some are involved in all twelve.

It is important as a Jedi to know your limitations and not just your strengths. If you are hopeless at one or more of the areas, that's no problem. I would choose not to focus on those so much, but to strengthen yourself in the areas where you can shine.

To help determine for yourself what area(s) you want to focus your energies on for improving yourself as a Jedi on your path to mastery, I suggest that you look at a couple of things. One, areas where you have, experience, strengths and skills, and secondly, where do your passions lie?

It is at the intersections of passions and skills that you would do well to focus your energies and other resources, such as time and sometimes money.

You may also find that your passions change over time. You might have had a love for the healing arts at one time in your life, but your passion for it has waned of late or you have found a different area even more enjoyable to move into.

I find most of the areas appealing, but I am only truly skilled and experienced in a few. That number is further cut down by my life situation. If you would love to learn a form of martial arts and to teach it to others, but you do not have a suitable dojo to go to in your town, you will most likely have to put your energies elsewhere.

If you are someone who hasn't yet found what truly inspires and motivates you, don't despair. Consulting an astrologer or other type of counselor could help you uncover what they are. There are many books devoted to this as well and there are resources such as the Myers-Briggs Personality Test that you could take in order to narrow things down, and you can always turn to meditation for the answers.

We sometimes forget that we can ask our family and friends for their opinions, when it is hard for us to see ourselves objectively. Other people can often be a mirror by which we can see ourselves more clearly.

For those of you who are discouraged because you haven't yet realized where your true path lies, there are a few things you can keep in mind.

Sometimes we are walking our path and don't know it or don't accept it as our path. Sometimes we find ourselves in a life situation that seems to be nowhere near what we envision or envisioned for ourselves. This is tough; no question about it, but the only way to get through something is to go through it. You can't go around, under or over something like this. Going through it is the only way, and the only way it can be a pleasant experience is through acceptance that this is what is meant to be for now.

Secondly, if you start down a path and find it's been a mistake, look at it in the positive. Now you know a path not to take in the future, which brings you closer to your true path.

A third thing I will say to those who are discouraged is to recall the story of the man who started Kentucky Fried Chicken; Col. Sanders. Did you know that he started his world famous franchise with his first retirement check at the age of 65? It's never too late to find your way. Keep at it; those who practice the Jedi path don't give up.

In the next chapter, we'll investigate how to live your path and take things to the next level.

Chapter Five: Living Your Path

Living your path—what does that mean? Many people live their life with very little reflection. Jedi don't do this. We reflect and adjust to make improvements, but more than that, we have a higher purpose for our existence. We are not content to merely live our life and hope for the best. We don't want to just get by. We want to live a life of excellence and one of service; one of mastery. Living our path means just this; that we put all of our effort into it, 110 percent.

Once we have discovered our path, it's time to put away silly, idle occupations and preoccupations. Most of our time should be spent doing our thing—living our path. Yes, there should be time for recreation, but many Jedi find recreation in what it is we are passionate about, and that involves the things that have to do with our chosen path.

When we are doing what we are passionate about and are caught up in it, we lose track of time and love every minute of it. This is called being in flow, or a Jedi might call it being at one with the Force. This happens to athletes who are performing at the top level of their game, to musicians, writers, anyone who is doing what they love and putting everything into it with pure focus.

When I was younger, I played varsity soccer. I recall a couple of games in particular where I was in flow. I could do no wrong. I played flawlessly. I was at one with the Force. It was inspiring to me and to those who witnessed it. The more this sort of thing happens, the closer we are to mastery.

Think back on your life so far. Did you experience being in flow, being at one with the Force at times? If you did, ask yourself some questions. What were the circumstances? Was it a fluke, or was something else going on at the time? The answers to these questions can point the way to reproducing such effect in your activities today. Often it is produced by letting go of the things that we cling to like day to day worries and cares.

Exercise:

Find a place where you can sit for ten or fifteen minutes undisturbed.

Ask yourself, how can I focus 100 percent on what I have chosen to do right now? Do I need to meditate in order to relax enough to let go completely? Reflect and see what it is you are preoccupied with at the moment. What are some things that are dragging on your mind, body or spirit?

Now take a few deep breaths. Visualize the things that you are worried about as being at the end of strings that are attached to your mind and perhaps some parts of your body. See and feel them tugging on you, pulling you this way and that. How does this make you feel, with all these demands pulling at your mind, body and energy?

Now visualize yourself taking a pair of scissors and cutting one of the strings. Feel the demands of that string, and the worry attached to it, fall away. How does this feel? Now, one by one, cut each of the strings until they are all gone. It doesn't even matter if you know what all the strings represent, just cut them off and let go.

Most people get a feeling of relaxation and liberation when they do this. If you don't, that's okay too. Not every exercise is going to work for everybody all the time.

I suggest doing this exercise at least three times per week for six months, either in the morning when you get up, or at dusk.

If you are keeping a journal, it would be a good idea to keep track of your results to these exercises. Note if you were or were not better able to focus after the exercise. Also, if you have a breakthrough with this or another exercise, write it down so you can return later to refresh yourself with the records, especially what worked well for you. This also goes for events of successes and less successful events in your daily life as you strive to live your path to the fullest.

Again, as Jedi, if we are to improve, we must reflect on our life, words and deeds often. This is how we become aware of what needs improvement.

What do we do when we are living our path and the road gets bumpy? I have some tips that may help you get through those times.

- Your path, no doubt, involves other people. Learn to ask others for help or even lean on others temporarily when things get tough.
- Know that everyone loses momentum or passion from time to time; we even lose interest sometimes. Every task has its boring components. Sometimes we just have to buckle down and just do what's next.
- When you are feeling overwhelmed, make a list and put your tasks in order of priority or highlight the tasks that need to be done more immediately and start doing and crossing off.
- When you have hit a plateau, it might be time to invest in more education or training. This can be scary for those who haven't had to do it in a while or ever. If it makes sense and you can afford the time and expense, it might be necessary and what you need to do next to stay on your path.

Chapter Six: The Struggle Part Two

It can be argued that life is circular, or a spiral. We're going along in life, our progress is good, we are living our path as Jedi, and boom! We hit a metaphorical brick wall that sets us back.

You might find yourself asking, what just happened? I was getting it; I was on my way to mastery. How can it be that I'm experiencing the same problem I thought I had gotten past long ago?

That's life, and we're not masters, yet. Life tests us, people test us. If this were not so, we couldn't become stronger and more skilled. One of the original ideas about Satan was that of the adversary, not pure evil, but an idea or energy that served the Force (or God's will) to test humankind so that we may improve and become more Godlike.

I was once caught in a negative cycle that was so intense that I nearly lost my mind and my life as well. After that, the negative periods still came, some stronger and some less so, but always the tests and always the struggle. Each of us has a dark side to our nature and sometimes the brighter we burn, the darker the darkness is. To light a candle is to cast a shadow. Someone once gave me a great complement, but added that I "mind my shadow." That's good advice for all of us.

Denial is a part of life. Harsh reality sometimes forces us to be in some level of denial most of the time, if only to keep our sanity in tact for the long haul. The path of truth means not denying for long, any part of our nature, lest we are really living a lie and that is a seed that can grow.

Exercise:

Think of what your shadow might be or how it makes itself known in your life. Can you see it or name it, or do you try to keep its reality from you? If you can see it or name it, don't judge. We all have darkness, but it is by objective observation and acknowledgement of it that it looses its power. Is it affecting your progress and your evolution?

A Note on Siths and the Dark Side of the Force

As we know, the goal of a Jedi is to serve others, but I'd like to expound on that a little now. A Jedi must also, in the interest of serving others, continuously work to improve their own life and skills. Sometimes we must serve ourselves before we can serve others. We just don't want to fall into the trap of serving only ourselves and extending that into manipulating others to serve us more and more.

This is the path of the Sith, as defined in Lucas' Star Wars Saga. Siths can be highly skilled. In fact, they have to be more skilled than most by far, but they are a negative element. Hitler was a Sith, but he was also a very confused individual. There are Siths that are much more highly skilled than Hitler ever was.

Keeping balance between light and darkness in the universe is one of the underling tasks of any Jedi, until the time when light is all that is, if ever there is such a time.

In summary, we will experience the same struggles over and over, sometimes under a different guise and at times to greater or lesser degrees, but realize that this is necessary. Accepting what we don't have control over is the only way to be at peace with life. We live in a chaotic world, but the one thing we can always control is how we choose to relate to the chaos.

Chapter Seven: The Power of Yielding

Unlike the struggles we encounter within ourselves, when dealing with other people, the struggle is different. We don't have control a lot of the time. For example, those who are close to us and those we encounter in our day-to-day lives are not always going to agree with us. A driver might honk his horn at you for something you aren't even doing, or you girl or boyfriend, husband or wife, son or daughter, might accuse you of something that's just not true.

These are good tests of your Jedi skills and your patience with yourself and others. Your reactions can be temporary indicators of where you are along your path, or they can be indications of a longer-term pattern.

Years ago, when I was much newer on the path of the Jedi, my reactions to accusations and criticisms included a lot of anger and sometimes retaliation. Today, in the face of criticism, I have learned to examine the facts and try to use the criticism to my advantage. I ask myself, is this criticism true? If it is to any degree, I make a mental note of it and look at myself in that light. I am able to stay calm and learn about myself to my longer term advantage. This is the power of yielding. Since I am more patient with myself, I am less prone to very angry reactions.

If the accusation or criticism is not true in the slightest, then I calmly explain that fact when the other person has stopped making noise. I have not succumbed to the temptation to blow up, start yelling in my defense and perhaps losing control of things to such a degree that the consequences are dire.

It is all too easy to fall into this trap. By defending ourselves and wanting to win the argument at all costs, we end up doing the opposite. We really lose. Technically we may have won the argument but we have lost the opportunity to take something negative and making it neutral or even a positive.

Think about when this has happened to you in the past. Did you make a bad situation worse? How could you have made it into something positive, or at least neutral?

Chapter Eight: Winning in Truth

The scenario that I just explained in Chapter Seven is part of what I call winning in truth. Yielding to the other's aggressive criticism or accusations is, in a sense, keeping small—or keeping your ego small.

If you stay small and learn from an experience, this is winning in truth. My quote at the beginning of Chapter One, "Sometimes when I lose, I really win," is from the movie, What Dreams May Come, staring Robin Williams. Robin's character in the movie had just yielded to his wife's despair and rather than letting her spend eternity in despair by herself, he decided he would spend it with her rather than living with himself knowing he left her alone. I won't spoil the ending completely, but what he does becomes a winning proposition.

This is similar to what Obi-Wan did when he yielded to Darth Vader in the original Star Wars movie. He accepted death, knowing that by so doing, he would become a much more powerful force for good.

In our daily lives we can practice "winning in truth." An example would be the wife who is being misunderstood by her husband or vice versa. They are criticized unfairly. So the one being criticized makes a strategic decision not to fight back this time; to let it go in the interest of keeping things from escalating into a big fight that could lead to more hateful things being said or done. By yielding now, he or she is preserving a peace that can lead to more harmony in the long run. Sometimes when we lose, we really win.

If someone honks at you in traffic for something you have or haven't done, you have the choice of honking back and perhaps making an obscene gesture at them, or you can stay calm, yield and avoid a possible escalation. In this case, you might win by keeping your calm, which is a more pleasant condition than being upset. You can win by not stooping to their level, and you might win by heading off a possible escalation of anger and associated actions.

Explaining, reading and understanding this is much easier than putting it into practice. But it is not impossible. This is what the path of truth is all about. Learning to know yourself honestly, finding your path as a Jedi, living your path and evolving into a stronger person. As a stronger people, we become a greater force for good in the universe.

May the light of the Force guide you and be with you always.

Appendix A – Extra Meditations

I.

Find a place and time that is quiet and free of distractions.

Get comfortable sitting or lying down. Take several deep breaths, breathing in through your nose and out through your mouth. Visualize while you are breathing in: see the green goodness of the earth filling you, or the white light of the divine filling you. Each time you breath out, visualize the dark, dingy red light of negativity escaping with your breath.

Once you have done this several times, visualize yourself sitting at the top of a hill in the shade under an enormous old tree. A gentle breeze is kissing your face and you hear the soft gurgling of a nearby stream. You notice how good it feels to be relaxed under this tree on top of this hill. Enjoy the feeling. Or you might in reality be having a hard time letting go of the anxieties of the day. Worried thoughts clutter your head and you are having trouble visualizing the natural beauty and ease of the meditation.

In either case, now you are going to say out loud or to yourself, "I am letting go of my worries. I am giving them up to the Force. The Force flows through me. The Force flows in me. It teaches me with its transformative power, a power greater than my daily concerns. It guides me to be still. My thoughts of worry do not have power over me. I am letting them go. The Force lifts me up to greater heights as a human. I am more than my mind and my thoughts, I am presence, I am the Force."

II.

Find a place and time that is quiet and free of distractions.

Get comfortable sitting or lying down. Take several deep breaths, breathing in through your nose and out through your mouth. As you breathe in, visualize the green goodness of the earth filling you, or the white light of the divine filling you, if you prefer. Each time you breath out, visualize the dark, dingy red light of negativity escaping with your breath.

Visualize yourself standing in a field or in the middle of a city. Experience yourself growing taller and taller. You are growing taller than the trees, taller than the tallest buildings. You are growing so tall that your head is in outer space. Notice how this feels. Does it give you a powerful feeling? Now you are growing so tall that you are passing by the various planets of our solar system. You are passing the Moon, Mars, Jupiter, Saturn, Uranus, Neptune, the dwarf planet, Pluto and beyond. Your feet are still on planet Earth.

Now you are detached from our Earth and are floating upright in space. You see above you the light of the divine. You reach up and draw some of the light down to you. It slowly touches your fingertips, permeates them, and very slowly fills your hands, arms, head and shoulders. The light fills your chest and torso, then moves down and fills your groin and legs, then finally your feet and the light moves outward from your feet and shoots down into infinity.

The light also shoots up from the top of your head into infinity. Then you move your right arm out, pointing away from yourself.

Your light shoots out sideways to infinity. You raise your left arm and your light shoots out to the left of you, out into infinity.

Experience this for a minute. Then slowly the light stops shooting outward and you experience your feet back on earth. Slowly you shrink back down, passing first Pluto, then Neptune, Uranus, Saturn, Jupiter, Mars, the Moon. You shrink back down to earth until you reach your original size.

Take a deep breath and open your eyes. What have you noticed about this experience? If it is of significance, record it in your journal.

Appendix B – The Jedi Guardians

As an example of the good works or real-life Jedi, the following is reproduced from the website of the Jedi Guardians (with permission).
http://www.jediguardians.com/

The Jedi Guardians are the premier lightsaber dueling group in the Washington D.C., Maryland and Northern Virginia area. We are a non-profit stage combat organization focused on giving back to the community. Our performances span charity events, community functions and fundraisers throughout the Washington DC / Baltimore area.

We perform for community organizations, fan groups and local charities. Contact us today to schedule an appearance.

We are a non-profit group and do not charge for appearances, to schedule a performance or if you require information on becoming a part of our team. Please contact us at the tab in the top menu.

Disclaimer: The Jedi Guardians is a non-profit fan operated website, and has no affiliation with Lucasfilm Ltd. No copyright infringement is intended by the use of these materials.

Notes:

Matthew Vossler

The third book of this series, *Jedi Mastery, Path of the Immortal*, will look at what it means to be a master and how to take that leap to mastery.

http://oaklightpublishing.com

Matthew Vossler

CPSIA information can be obtained at www.ICGtesting.com
Printed in the USA
BVOW031702021211

277467BV00001B/19/P